MATH 015

Mythical and Legendary Figures

Maritime Anthropology (MATH) a topic which covers prehistoric, historic and modern life, and inspirations derived from the world's oceans and the brave souls who have subsisted on and inhabited the surrounding environs of the sea.

MATH 015 Mythical and Legendary Figures focuses on the people and mythical figures who explored the world's oceans, sought new lands and developed maritime culture as it is currently known. Inspiring generations to travel, explore and strengthen their character to live in new and foreign locations. Mythology and Folklore, and Fables drawn from various geographic regions and chronological phases thant can be segmented into other modules for specific interests. Contact Skye Research for further information.

Research and module development

by

Yvonne-Cher Skye

Skye Research

Statement of Purpose

To create an educational program from which educators can create a program to sell to potential students as part of a maritime cultural experience. The intended audience can be variable from a one hour, one day seminar course to an 18 week course semester.

The actual lesson plans are at the discretion of the instructor. The materials available in this booklet are meant to be a reference point to assist the instructor in developing a foundation from which the intended course can be derived.

As this is in the early stages of production, all comments and suggestions for improvement are welcome.

Sincerely,

Yvonne-Cher Skye

Table of Contents

Summary

Objective:

Lecture on the topic of Myths that inspired artwork, cartographer and exploration.

Materials Needed:

Instructor: PowerPoint Presentation

Students: Journals, writing implements

Vocabulary introduced:

- giants
- halcyon days
- King Canute
- lorelei
- Mermaids
- selkies
- sirens

Background:

All of Maritime History began with the observation of the oceans and rivers by man.

Further specific lectures can be assigned module letters as the need arises.

Reference:

Seafaring Lore and Legend, Peter D. Jeans 2007

Wikipedia

Personal experiences

Personal research

Lesson Plan:

Introduce the terms and concepts via PowerPoint by using images and bulleted lists to convey the information. Dialogue with the students in a question and answer format.

Introduction:

Explain subject matter, and resource materials, with an eye on multimedia and hands-on instruction when materials are available.

Body:

- giants
- halcyon days
- King Canute
- lorelei
- Mermaids
- selkies
- sirens

Conclusion:

Direction on how instructor can conclude the module

Clean-Up:

Students take their things with them.

Learning sessions

Textbook reading chapters can be developed per the Instructor's chosen textbook or via their own manual dependent on scope of material intended to be covered in this course

Individual sections with dividers each focusing on one component of the content: All of the following will be determined by Instructor, module course outline gives examples of the following:

a. Learning outcomes

b. Session Information

c. Learning activities

d. Learning Resources

e. Evaluation Procedures

f. Timing and assignment

Course Outline

Catalog number: MATH 015   **Course Title:** Myths

Year: 2017   **Semester:**

Instructor: **Office Location:**

Office Hours:

Objectives of the course:

Explain myths and tall tales of maritime lore.

Explain and Identify myths and deities worshiped by maritime people.

Any measurable objectives that can be demonstrated by student.

Procedures for accomplishing these objectives:

Lectures

Class discussions

Analytic questions

Projects

Research papers

Use of visual and oral reports

Fields trips

Visiting lecturers

Student testimonials

Use of multimedia i.e. videos, audio recordings to exemplify topics

Student requirements for completion of the course:

Varies per instructor discretion and length of program

During introductory lecture, the instructor must list specific work students must complete in order to receive credit for the course

Student need to demonstrate the accomplishment of each objective, examples are as follows:

Read all the chapters in the textbook

Submit a research paper

Oral report on topic

Submit book report

Complete lab reports

Complete periodic quizzes

Complete mid-term exam

Complete final exam

Grading Practices:

Students will be graded using above methods, at the instructor's discretion

Relative importance of each item

Four quizzes: 40%

Two book reports 20%

Term paper 20%

Final exam 20%

Equals 100%

Rules Concerning student absence and lateness:

At the discretion of the instructor and student agreement

If marina, ship or school follows specific rules, then state explicitly

Textbook:

List author, title publisher, date of publication of any required texts, manuals

Weekly Outline Topics to be covered:

List topics in sequential order, examples included with this packet are:

Mermaids

Sirens

The Lorelei

Selkies

Halcyon Days

King Canute

List tests, quizzes, due dates for papers

Audio Visual Materials to be used:

List any visual elements to be used during course including:

PowerPoint presentations

Youtube videos

Photos

Graphs

Maps

List of supplementary readings:

MATH 015 Myths

List books, periodicals, articles which students should read in addition to text

Miscellaneous information:

Any information that will further clarify what is hoped to be achieved in the course and how you plan to achieve it.

Audio Visual Experience

Photos

Please see attached document entitled Photos.

These will be updated as research is continued.

Useful weblinks leading to images can be found on the following websites:

Websites on subject

http://www.merriam-webster.com/dictionary/archetype

https://skyeresearchygfi.wordpress.com/2016/06/15/math-marine-anthropology-015-summary/

https://skyeresearchygfi.wordpress.com/2016/09/03/math-015-youtube-channel/

Audio recordings, videos or script to explain each section

Youtube channel Playlist MATH 001 at this link:

https://www.youtube.com/playlist?

list=PLBHbcZSn310CUhmMTkHoPqJlylPpYw1Jr

Appendices

    Glossary

    Maps

    Artistic renderings

    Works Cited

Glossary

The purpose of this glossary is to provide terms that pertain to the current topic in this book and educational module. Each letter is separated onto its own page allowing for space on the bottom of each list for each student to write in terms that the instructor prefers to include in their course.

A

Aeolus is the God that is the keeper of the Winds, and lived on the island of Aeolia. Aeolus lived on the island with his wife, as well as his six sons and six daughters. Each son married one of each of their sisters. He was the founder of Aeolian race.

Alcyone is the daughter of Aeolous and the wife of Ceyx. She is the primary character in the Halcyon Days myth. She upon mourning the death of her husband in a shipwreck, threw herself into the sea. Her father changed her to a kingfisher so that she would live on, and seven days of the year when the ocean is still, so that she can lay her eggs.

C

Ceyx is the husband of Acylone. He was a King in Greek Mythology. He was killed in a shipwreck. He was transformed into a kingfisher in response to his wife trying to kill herself upon hearing of his death.

G

Giants are humanoid, who are of a significant size larger than the human population. They exist in almost every cultural mythos. Giants were encountered by Odysseus, Hercules, and Ancient mariners.

H

Halcyon days a period of peace and happiness, a period of calm weather during the weather solstice. In Greek Mythology, Alcyone who was the daughter of Aeolus and wife of Ceyx. When her husband died in a shipwreck, Alcyone threw herself into the sea whereupon gods transformed them both into halcyon birds (kingfishers). When Alcyone made her nest on the beach, waves threatened to destroy it. Aeolus restrained the winds and made the waves be calm during seven days in each year, so she could lay her eggs. These became known as the halcyon days when storms never occur.

K

King Canute is Cnut the Great (Old Norse: Knútr inn ríki; c. 995 – 12 November 1035), also known as Canute – whose father was Sweyn Forkbeard (which gave him the patronym Sweynsson, Old Norse: Sveinsson) – was King of Denmark, England and Norway; together often referred to as the North Sea Empire. His Coronation was in London, England January 6, 1017. He united the Danes and the English under wealth and custom rather than through brutality.

Kingfisher in the Greek Myth regarding the Halcyon days, the bodies of Acylone and Ceyx are transformed into kingfisher rather than death. A brightly colored bird that has a large head and short tail. It feeds mainly on fish.

L

Lorelei is

1. a quasilegendary nymph of the Rhine who lured sailors to shipwreck on her rock by singing;
2. a Germanic myth;
3. a creation of Clemens Brentano in a poem of 1800.

M

Mermaid a fictitious or mythical half-human sea creature with the head and trunk of a woman and the tail of a fish, conventionally depicted as beautiful and with long flowing golden hair.

Merman is a fictitious or mythical half-human sea creature with the head and trunk of a man and the tail of a fish, conventionally depicted as beautiful and with long flowing golden hair.

Merpeople is a race of fictitious or mythical half-human sea creatures.

S

Selkies a mythical creature that takes the form of a seal in the water. It takes the form of a human when it walks on land.

Sirens each of a number of women or winged creatures whose singing lured unwary sailors onto rocks.

Maps

will be added per the request and special requirements of the instructor.

Artistic renderings

will be added per the request and special requirements of the instructor.

Works Cited

http://www.merriam-webster.com/dictionary

http://www.wikitionary.com/kingfisher

http://www.wikitionary.com

Bibliography

The following is a list of books that I have referenced throughout my research for all of the volumes contained within the MATH collection: More will be added as my research continues. Each letter will be started on a new page to allow for spacing below each entry so that instructors or researchers can add their own titles.

#

20.000 Leagues under the Sea by Jules Verne 1962

A

A Guide to Shipwreck Sites along the Oregon Coast by Victor C. West 1984

A Mariner's Guide to Radiofacsimile Weather Charts by Dr. Joseph M. Bishop 1994

A World of My Own by Robin Knox-Johnston. New York: W.W. Norton & Co., 1992.

Adrift by Steven Callahan New York: Ballantine Books, 1996.

Albatross by Deborah Scaling Kiley and Meg Noonan. New York: Hiughton Mifflin, 1994.

Atlas of Hawaii by Juvik and Juvik

B

Basic Hawaiiana 1990

Battleship Missouri by Ronn Ronck 1999

C

Common Seashore Life of Southern California by Joel Hedgpeth and Sam Hinton 1961

Cruising Guide to California's Channel Islands by Brian Fagan 1983

D

Desolation Island by Patrick O'Brien. Glasgow; William Collins & Sons & Co., 1978.

Directory of Historical Repositories in Hawaii

Diver's Almanac Hawaii by Rock Baker

Diving Knowledge Workbook PADI

E

Emma Naca Rooke (1836 – 1885 Beloved Queen of Hawaii by Russell E. Benton

F

Feathered Gods and Fishhooks by Patrick Vinton Kirch 1985

Folk Wisdom of Hawaii by Ann Kondo Corum

G

Ghost Dog and Other Hawaiian Legends by George Thomas Armitage and Henry Pratt

Great Shipwrecks and Castaways Edited by Charles Neider 1989

Gulliver's Travels by Jonathan Swift 1999

H

Handy Hawaiian Dictionary by Henry P. Judd 1995

Haunted Hawaiian Nights by Lopaka Kapanui 2005

Hawaii Museums and Cultural Attractions

Hawaiian Legends Index Vol 1 A-J

Hawaiian Legends Index Vol 2 K

Hawaiian Legends Index Vol 3 L - Y

Hawaiian Legends of Ghosts

Hawaiian Legends of Old Honolulu

Hawaiian Legends of Volcanoes

Hawaiian National Bibliography Vol I 1780 - 1830

Hawaiian National Bibliography Vol II 1831 - 1850

Hawaiian National Bibliography Vol III 1851 – 1880

Hawaiian National Bibliography Vol IV 1881- 1900

Hawaiian Proverbs and Riddles by Henry Judd

History Makers of Hawaii A Biographical Dictionary A list of 500 people who have died that have contributed to Hawaii's History by Day A Grove

I

Ice Bird by David Lewis. New York: W. W. Norton& Co., 1976.

In Gramma's Wake: Girl Stella's Voyage to Cuba . Suffolk England: Seafarer Books, 1970.

L

Looking for a ship by John McPhee. New York: Farrar, Straus 7 Giroux, 1990.

M

Mapping the lands and waters of Hawaii by Moffat & Fitzpatrick

Maps of the Ancient Sea Kings by Charles H. Hapgood 1979

Maui Mischievous Hero by Barbary Lyons 1969

Myths and Legends of Hawaii & Pacific

O

Oahu Revealed by Andrew Doughty 2011

Oceania Native Cultures of Australia and the Pacific Islands Vol I Douglas L. Oliver 1989

Oceania Native Cultures of Australia and the Pacific Islands Vol II Douglas L. Oliver 1989

P

PADI Open Water Diver Manual

PADI Adventures in Diving

PADI Divemaster Manual

Pele and Hiiaka A myth from Hawaii by Nathaniel Bright Emerson

Portland's Lost Waterfront by Barney Blacklock 2012

R

Rescue in the Pacific by Tony Farrington. New York: International Marine,/McGraw 1996

Robinson Crusoe by Daniel Defoe 1957

S

Sailing for Beginners by Moulton H. Farnham 1967

Schooner from Windward Two Centuries of Hawaiian Interisland Shipping by Thomas Liffin 1983

Sea and Earth: The Life of Rachel Carson by Phillip Sterling 1970

Seafaring Lore and Legend by Peter D. Jeans 2007

Shackleton's Boat Journey by F.A. Worsley . New York: W. W. Norton & Co., 1978

Silent Spring by Rachel Carson 1962

Silent World by Jacques-Yves Cousteau 1953

Solomon Mysteries by Marius Boirayan 2009

Supernatural Hawaii by Judi Thompson 2009

T

The Breath of Angels by John Beattie. Dobbs Ferry, N.Y. :Sheridan House, 1997.

The Caine Mutiny by Herman Wouk. New York: Doubleday , 1951.

The Captain Encyclopedia by Robison

The Encyclopedia of Recreational Diving PADI

The Hawaiian Annotated Bibliography

The Hawaiian Canoe by Holmes

The History of Pirates by Angus Konstam 2002

The Illustrated Atlas of Hawaii

The Journal of Captain James Cook III The Voyage of the Resolution and Discovery

The Life of Captain James Cook by John Cawte Beaglehole 1974

The Living Sea by Jacques-Yves Cousteau 1963

The Loss of the S.S. Titanic by Lawrence Beesley. Boston & New York: Houghton Mifflin, 1912.

The Menehune of Polynesia and other mythical little people of Oceania by Katherine Luomala

The Night Marchers by Hoyt

The Pacific Islands: environment and Society by Moshe Rapaport 1999

The Pirates Own Book by Marine Research Society 1993

The Raft by Robert Trumbull . Maryland: Naval Institute Press, 1992.

The Riddle of the Bermuda Triangle Edited by Martin Ebon 1975

The Seaworthy Offshore Sailboat by John Vigor 2001

The Shipwreck that Saved Jamestown by Lorri Glover and Daniel Blake Smith New York, Henry Holt and Company, LLC 2008

The United States Power Squadron Boating Course 2004

The Visual Encyclopedia of Nautical Terms Under Sail by Crown Publishers, New York 1978

Thirty Years from home: or a Voice from the Maiin Deck. By Samuel Leech. Boston: Tappen, Whittemore and Mason 1843

Treasure Island by Roubert Louis Stevenson 1980

Two Years Before the Mast by Richard Henry Dana. Boston: Houghton, Mifflin, 1995.

U

Unbroken by Laura Hillenbrand New York, Delacort Press 2014

V

Vaka Moana Voyages of the Ancestors by K.R. Howe

Vikings of the Sunrise (Vikings of the Pacific) by Sir Peter Henry Buck 1985

Voyages to Hawaii before 1860

W

Who's Who in Pacific Navigation by Dunmore

Back Page

For further sources and information on the research conducted on this topic, it is recommended that you order the supplemental materials entitled notes and photos.

We have made every effort to trace copyright holders, but if errors or omissions are brought to our attention we shall be pleased to publish corrections in future editions of this book.

www.ingramcontent.com/pod-product-compliance
Lightning Source LLC
Chambersburg PA
CBHW081604280526
45788CB00011B/3540